Amazing BIRDS

by Brenda Williams

ticktock

Copyright © ticktock Entertainment Ltd 2007

First published in Great Britain in 2007 by ticktock Media Ltd,
2 Orchard Business Centre, North Farm Road, Tunbridge Wells, Kent, TN2 3XF

ticktock project editor: Ruth Owen
ticktock project designer: Sara Greasley
With thanks to: Trudi Webb, Sally Morgan and Elizabeth Wiggans

ISBN 978-1-84696-072-7 pbk

Printed in China

Picture credits (t=top; b=bottom; c=centre; l=left; r=right):
Corbis: 7tl, 7r, 10c, 20tl, 22c. FLPA: 6tl, 8tl, 9 main, 9tl, 15cl, 17t, 17r, 21b, 24b, 25t, 25b, 29cl, 30b.
Nature Picture Library: 26, 27. Shutterstock: OFC, 1, 2, 3, 4tl, 4–5 main, 4b, 5t, 7bl, 8c, 8b, 9tr, 10tl, 10br, 11t, 11b, 12tl, 12c, 12b,
13, 14tl, 14–15c, 14cr, 14cl, 14b, 15tl, 15tr, 15cr, 15b, 16tl, 16, 18, 19, 22tl, 23, 24tl, 28, 29r, 30tl, 31, OBC.
Superstock: 5b, 20 main, 21t. ticktock image archive: map page 6, globe page 22.

Every effort has been made to trace copyright holders, and we apologise in advance for any omissions. We would be
pleased to insert the appropriate acknowledgments in any subsequent edition of this publication.

Contents

Words that look
bold like this
are in the glossary.

What is a bird?

Birds have something that no other animals have – feathers! Other animals have wings, and other animals lay eggs, but no other animals have feathers. A bird's feathers help to keep it warm.

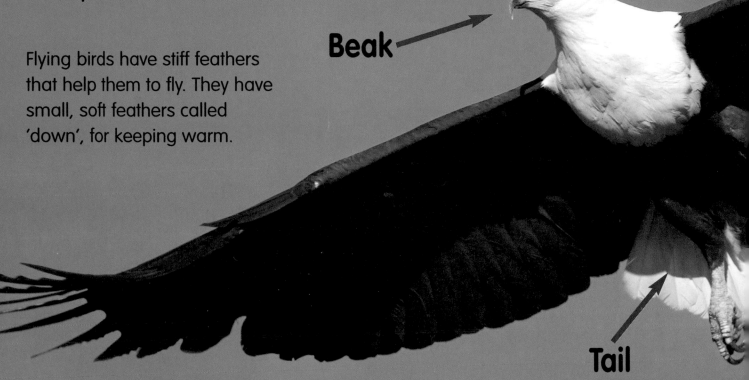

Water birds, such as ducks, have waterproof feathers.

Flying birds have stiff feathers that help them to fly. They have small, soft feathers called 'down', for keeping warm.

Beak

Tail

Millions of years ago, prehistoric **reptiles** lived on Earth. These reptiles were the **ancestors** of birds.

Birds lay eggs like reptiles, but birds are **endothermic** animals, like **mammals**.

Scales

Birds have scales on their legs and feet, and claws like reptiles.

Flying feathers

Wing

Claws

Birds can be tiny, like the hummingbirds in this picture, or huge like an ostrich.

The ostrich is the biggest bird in the world. An adult male can be 2.5 metres tall!

AMAZING BIRD FACT
An ostrich is too heavy to fly, but it can run fast. Its top speed is 70 km/h.

Bird habitats

A habitat is the place where a plant or an animal lives. Birds live in warm places, such as **rainforests**, and cold places such as the Antarctic. Many birds live close to people, in cities or around farms.

This robin has built a nest on a shelf in a garden shed!

Birds live in most of the world's habitats.

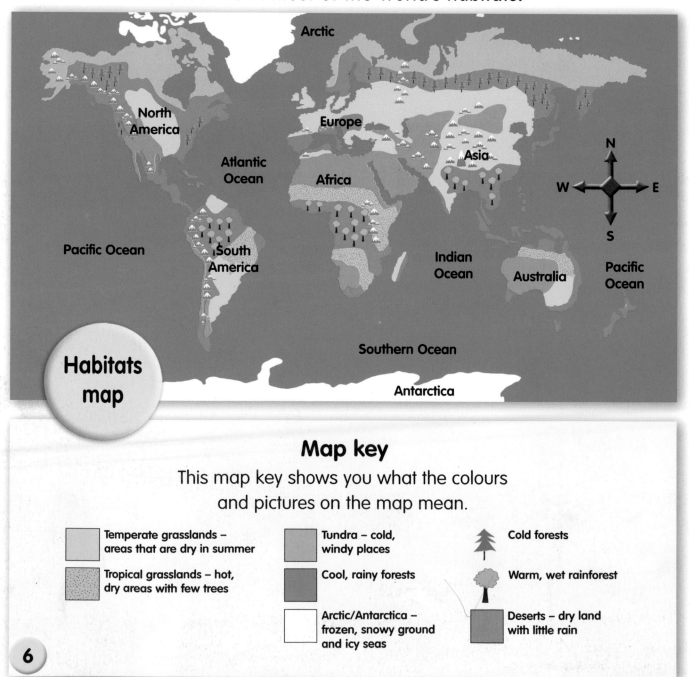

Habitats map

Map key

This map key shows you what the colours and pictures on the map mean.

Temperate grasslands – areas that are dry in summer

Tropical grasslands – hot, dry areas with few trees

Tundra – cold, windy places

Cool, rainy forests

Arctic/Antarctica – frozen, snowy ground and icy seas

Cold forests

Warm, wet rainforest

Deserts – dry land with little rain

Emperor penguins live in the Antarctic – the coldest place on Earth.

Emperor penguins are the biggest type of penguin.

Water-loving birds live beside rivers, lakes or the sea. Gulls and other seabirds build their nests on cliffs. They gather together in big **colonies**.

Macaws live in warm rainforests.

This is a gannet nesting colony.

Wings and flying

Birds have very light bodies. Their bones are **hollow**, but very strong. Birds have powerful muscles to beat their wings up and down. Flying is hard work, so birds spend a lot of time eating.

Swifts catch insects in the air.

You can tell from a wing shape how a bird flies. A swift has long, pointed wings for fast flying.

A buzzard has broad wings for gliding and soaring high in the sky.

Buzzards fly high looking out for food, such as mice, on the ground.

AMAZING BIRD FACT
A robin's short wings are good for quick short flights from place to place catching bugs to eat.

The wandering albatross's wingspan is four metres.

A pair of wandering albatrosses.

The wandering albatross has the biggest **wingspan** in the bird kingdom. It spends most of its life flying over the ocean. It flies to land when it is time to **mate**, lay eggs and raise its young.

Many baby birds fly without being shown how. They tumble out of the nest, spread their wings, and fly. Other babies need to practise.

This baby albatross is practising flapping its wings.

Mum meets dad

Most birds **breed** every year, usually in the spring. Some birds stay together as a pair for life. Other birds have a new partner each year. Some females will have chicks with more than one male in the same year.

A male and a female swan pair for life.

Tail

Some male birds have colourful feathers to attract females. The male peacock shows off to the female peahen by spreading his tail feathers like a fan.

Many male birds sing to attract a female to their **territory**. They defend their territory and their female by chasing away other males.

Peacock tail feathers are the longest feathers of any bird.

Some pairs of birds perform a dance together before they mate. The male blue-footed booby dances for the female. He shows her his blue feet and whistles.

The male booby spreads his wings and puts his beak in the air as part of his dance.

AMAZING BIRD FACT
To attract a mate the male frigate bird puffs out his bright red throat like a balloon.

Eggs and nests

Many female birds make a nest on their own. Others are helped by their partner. Some birds make the nest before they mate – some do it afterwards. Next, the female bird lays her eggs in the nest.

This female swan is collecting leaves to put in her nest.

Some birds make nests from grass, twigs or leaves. The flamingo makes a nest of mud with a hollow top.

The white stork's nest is made of sticks. The storks add more sticks every year, so the nest gets bigger and bigger!

The female flamingo lays one or two eggs.

The female stork lays up to four eggs in her nest.

Adult woodpecker

Chick

This great spotted woodpecker makes a nest in a hole in a tree.

This bald eagle is sitting on her eggs.

Female birds sit on the eggs, to keep them warm. This is called **incubation**. Some males help with this job, too, and they bring food for the female.

Chicks **hatch** from the eggs. Many chicks are helpless. Mum and dad bring food for the chicks.

What is a life cycle?

A life cycle is all the different **stages** and changes that a plant or animal goes through in its life. This diagram shows a bird life cycle.

A robin chick eats about 140 bugs, spiders and worms a day!

1 An adult male and female bird meet and mate.

6

This is the life cycle of a robin.

When they are ready to go off on their own, the chicks leave the nest. Some parents teach their chicks how to fly. This is a picture of a young robin.

5

The parents bring the chicks food to eat. Some birds remove their chicks' poo from the nest, too!

Amazing bird life cycles

In this book we are going to find out about some amazing animal life cycles – from the record-breaking Arctic tern to the tricky killdeer.

Arctic tern

Killdeer

2

The female lays eggs in a nest.

Robin's live in Europe, North Africa and parts of Asia.

3

The female sits on the eggs to keep them warm. Some male birds bring the female food while she does this.

4

The eggs hatch. Many chicks are blind and have no feathers when they hatch.

This is a southern ground hornbill. It feeds on the ground.

Hornbill

Hornbills live in the forests of Africa and Asia. The hornbill uses its large beak, or bill, to eat fruit, and to catch insects, lizards and snakes.

Most types of hornbill find their food in the trees, but some feed on the ground.

This great Indian hornbill lives in trees.

LIFE CYCLE FACTS
The female hornbill lays up to six eggs. The chicks hatch in about 30 to 40 days.

Hornbills nest in holes in trees. The female lays her eggs, then shuts herself inside. She blocks the entrance with a wall made from droppings mixed with mud and squashed fruit.

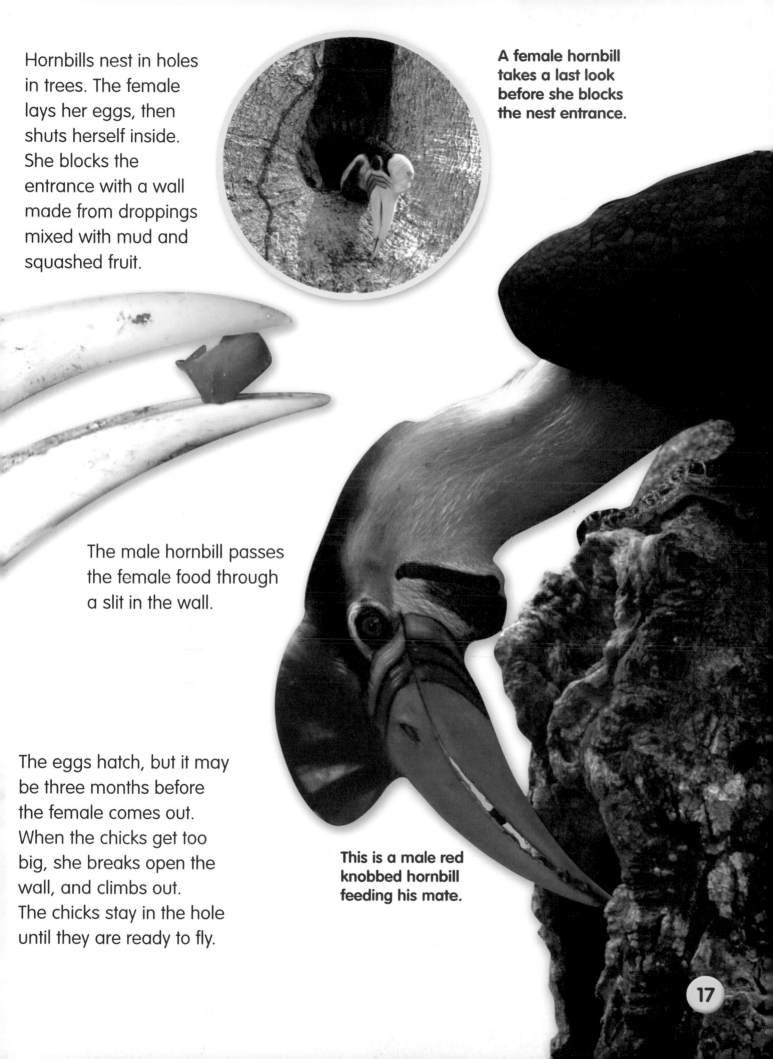

A female hornbill takes a last look before she blocks the nest entrance.

The male hornbill passes the female food through a slit in the wall.

The eggs hatch, but it may be three months before the female comes out. When the chicks get too big, she breaks open the wall, and climbs out. The chicks stay in the hole until they are ready to fly.

This is a male red knobbed hornbill feeding his mate.

AMAZING BIRD LIFE CYCLE

Killdeer

Killdeers live on grasslands. They eat worms, beetles, grasshoppers and snails. Killdeers nest on the ground where there are lots of dangers – chicks can run as soon as they hatch!

A killdeer will run at a horse or cow to scare it and stop the big animal stepping on its eggs.

The killdeer's eggs are **camouflaged** to hide them from egg-eating **predators**.

Killdeer chicks have feathers as soon as they hatch.

Eggs

On the grassland, there is nowhere to hide. The chicks have to sit still in the grass.

To protect its family from predators, such as foxes, the killdeer has a trick. It drags one of its wings on the ground so it looks injured.

The fox follows the killdeer thinking it will get an easy meal. The killdeer leads the fox away from the nest then flies away. The chicks wait, keeping very still and quiet, until mum returns.

LIFE CYCLE FACTS
The female killdeer normally lays four eggs. The chicks hatch after about 25 days.

**Penguin pairs stay
together for years.**

Emperor penguin

Penguins cannot fly. They use their wings as flippers for swimming in the sea. Emperor penguins do not build nests. After mating, the female lays one egg. The male holds the egg on his feet to keep it warm.

The new chick is warm on Dad's feet!

The female goes off to sea to catch fish. Sometimes emperor penguins walk for 100 kilometres to get to the sea.

All winter the male cares for the egg. In spring, the egg hatches and the female returns from the sea with food for the chick.

LIFE CYCLE FACTS
The female emperor penguin lays one egg. The chick hatches after about 65 days.

When the egg has hatched, the male and female take it in turns to care for the chick and go fishing.

Until their adult feathers grow, the chicks cannot swim. After four or five months, the chicks' feathers grow and they are able to go to sea to find food on their own.

The parent penguin coughs up partly digested fish from its throat, for the chick.

Arctic terns catch fish
by plunging into
the sea.

Arctic tern

The Arctic tern is the champion bird traveller.
Each year, this small seabird **migrates** from
the Arctic to Antarctica, and back again. Arctic
terns fly about 35,000 kilometres around the
world every year.

Arctic terns have two summers every year.

When it is winter in the
north of the world, it is
summer in the south.
Arctic terns fly south
to escape the cold
northern winter.
When the southern
summer ends, they
fly north again.

ARCTIC TERN MIGRATION ROUTE

Arctic

Atlantic Ocean

Africa

South America

Antarctica

This map shows the Arctic tern's migration
from north to south and back again.

Arctic terns pair
for life. They mate
and lay their
eggs in the Arctic.

Chick

The parent terns raise their chicks during the short Arctic summer. When it's time to fly south, the parent terns guide the youngsters to show them the way.

LIFE CYCLE FACTS
The female Arctic tern lays two or three eggs. The chicks hatch after about 24 days.

The parents bring the chicks fish to eat.

The satin bower bird has blue-black feathers and bright, blue eyes.

Bower bird

Bower birds live in Australia and New Guinea. The male makes a little archway, called a bower, to attract a mate. He puts colourful things such as stones, bones, feathers or shells inside the bower. He makes a garden, too!

The male dances in and out of his bower. Females visit several bowers before deciding on a mate.

Bower

LIFE CYCLE FACTS

The female satin bower bird lays two or three eggs. The chicks hatch between 15 and 30 days.

Sometimes males steal decorations from each other's bowers!

This bird is taking a piece of blue Lego!

Satin bower birds like blue. A male may collect blue drinking straws, bits of blue plastic, even ballpoint pens!

Male

Female

This is a pair of great bower birds.

After mating, the female bower bird makes a saucer-shaped nest for her eggs. The male doesn't help – he is more interested in his bower.

25

Tailorbird

The tailorbird lives in south Asia. It makes a very unusual nest! Just as a tailor sews cloth to make clothes, the tailorbird sews leaves together to make a nest.

Tailorbirds don't mind people. Some nest in gardens.

First the tailorbird chooses a long, wide leaf. Using its beak as a needle, it sews the edges of the leaf together to make a bag shape.

Leaf

26

For thread, the bird uses plant fibres or spider's web. It makes neat, tight stitches. Inside the leaf-bag, the bird makes a cosy nest of spider's web, bits of string – anything soft.

Soft nest material

LIFE CYCLE FACTS
The female tailorbird lays between three and five eggs. The chicks hatch after 12 days.

Stitches

This tailorbird nest has dried out. The chicks have left.

Leaf bag

The female sits on the eggs to incubate them. Both parents feed the chicks on insects and spiders.

Puffins eat fish – they can carry 10 small fish sideways in their beaks.

Puffin

The puffin is a seabird that nests on cliffs. Puffins are excellent swimmers. Male and female puffins do a courtship dance – they bob heads and touch beaks. Then they mate out at sea.

A courtship dance.

The puffin pair dig a nest **burrow,** using their beaks and feet. Some puffins nest inside empty rabbit holes.

LIFE CYCLE FACTS

The female puffin lays one egg. The chick hatches after about 40 days.

Burrow entrance

Inside the burrow the female lays one egg. Both parents incubate the egg and catch fish for the chick when it hatches.

When the chick is six weeks old, the parents leave it. After a week on its own, the chick leaves the burrow.

Nest material

Puffin chick

The chick rushes to the sea, usually at night, when there are few predators around. Rats and seagulls will kill puffin chicks.

That's amazing!

Birds are very good parents. They care for their eggs and chicks by building them a safe, cosy home and bringing them food. But did you know that there is one bird that's a very lazy parent!

Swallows stick their nests to houses or cave walls, using their gummy spit as glue.

The cuckoo lays its egg in the nest of another bird and then leaves it. The other bird does not notice the strange egg. The cuckoo chick hatches after 12 days and pushes the other eggs or chicks out of the nest.

The cuckoo gets all the food and is soon bigger than its new parents!

Cuckoo chick

Wagtail adult

Nest

Ostrich egg

Chicken egg

African weaver birds nest in colonies. Each pair of birds weaves a nest from grass and leaves.

An ostrich egg is the biggest egg in the bird kingdom. A hummingbird's egg is the smallest – it's about the size of a pea!

AMAZING BIRD FACT
Ostrich chicks are looked after by their dad – mum doesn't help at all!

Glossary

ancestors – Parents, grandparents, great-grandparents – all the earlier individuals that came before.

breed – To mate and have babies.

burrow – Tunnels and holes under the ground where some animals live.

camouflaged – Having colours, marks or a shape that hides an animal from predators, and its prey.

colonies – Large groups.

endothermic – Animals whose body temperature stays the same no matter how hot or cold the air or water is around them. You are endothermic!

hatch – When a baby bird or animal breaks out of its egg.

hollow – Something empty inside.

incubation – Keeping an egg warm after laying, and before it hatches.

mammals – Endothermic animals with hair, that feed their babies milk.

mate – When a male and female animal meet and have babies.

migrates – Travels a long way to find food or a place to breed.

predators – Animals which hunt and kill other animals for food.

rainforests – Forests of tall trees in warm places with lots of rain.

reptiles – Animals with scales such as snakes, lizards and crocodiles.

stages – Different times of an animal's life when the animal changes.

territory – An area or place where an animal feeds and breeds.

wingspan – The distance from the tip of one wing to the tip of the other.

Index